simple stunning wedding
FLOWERS

Practical Ideas and Inspiration for Your Bouquet, Ceremony, and Centerpieces

Karen Bussen

Photographs by **William Geddes**

STEWART, TABORI & CHANG • NEW YORK

For my mother Linda Mikhael

Editor: Jennifer Levesque
Designer: Susi Oberhelman
Production Manager: Jane Searle

Library of Congress Cataloging-in-
Publication Data

Bussen, Karen.
  Simple stunning wedding flowers / by
Karen Bussen ; photographs by William
Geddes.
    p. cm.
  Includes index.
  ISBN-13: 978-1-58479-539-1
  ISBN-10: 1-58479-539-5
  1. Wedding decorations. 2. Flower
arrangement. 3. Bridal bouquets. I. Title.

SB449.5.W4B87 2006
745.92'6—dc22   2006009488

Published in 2006 by
Stewart, Tabori & Chang
An imprint of Harry N. Abrams, Inc.

The text of this book was composed in
Helvetica Neue and New Caledonia

Printed and bound in China

10 9 8 7 6 5 4 3 2 1

HNA ▪▪▪▪▪
harry n. abrams, inc.
a subsidiary of La Martinière Groupe

115 West 18th Street | New York, NY 10011
www.hnabooks.com

contents

INTRODUCTION
Your Wedding in Full Bloom

Flowers truly do seem to speak to us. They offer cheer, comfort, delight, and joy with their colors, perfumes, and shapes. But surely the lucky blossoms chosen to adorn a wedding celebration share the most festive of messages, expressing the happiness and romance of such a special day.

Perhaps you already have a vision of your own wedding flowers. Or maybe you're just beginning to dream about the possibilities. Whether you imagine rustic sunflowers, tailored roses, or exotic orchids, there is much to consider concerning which blooms will best suit your ceremony and festivities.

In my years working directly with brides as a designer, florist, and planner, I've learned a great deal about wedding flowers. I had never had a green thumb when I was growing up in Ohio; I'd even managed to kill a friend's cactus (or three) while plant-sitting when she was out of town.

However, I came to love working with flowers when I was managing a restaurant located near the wholesale flower market in Manhattan. I made a deal with the owner of the restaurant: I'd arrange the flowers if he'd pay for the cost of the blooms. It was a wonderful opportunity to learn and practice without the expense of buying costly varieties myself.

Flowers

are love's

truest

language.

—Park Benjamin,
Nineteenth-century American journalist

Today's brides are embracing color like never before. This vibrant, tailored bouquet of red roses and anemones makes a powerfully chic, romantic statement.

Later, when a couple who were regular customers at the restaurant decided to host their wedding reception in the dining room, my career as a wedding designer began. Armed with a bundle of inspiration but not much experience, I waited until ten o'clock the night before the celebration to start making the centerpieces, because I wanted them to be fresh and perfect! I can still remember working all through the night, surrounded by hundreds of beautiful white blossoms in my little apartment. Sure, I was tired, but I was so happy!

Over the years, I've spent countless very early mornings shopping in New York City's flower district for the best blooms and making notes of what's in season from week to week. The exquisite array of colors, fragrances, and textures always astonishes me. To this day, one of my favorite activities is taking a bride-to-be to the market with me a few weeks before her wedding. Together we marvel at the beauty and abundance of blossoms, and we have fun experimenting with shapes and shades as we select flowers for her bouquets and centerpieces.

I hope you'll use this book as a tool as you imagine and bring to life your own vision. My goal is to help you learn where to splurge, where to save, and how to create mood with color, texture, and style.

The principles of simple stunning design will help you streamline your ideas and your communications with floral professionals. If you're planning to fashion your own centerpieces or bouquets, you'll find lots of advice on everything from containers to flower substitutes for your budget and season. Every photograph in this book was created to illustrate and inspire with practical yet enchanting ideas.

If you'd like more information about where to find the items featured in this book, take a look at the Resource Guide on page 107. Also, look for my planning workbook called *Simple Stunning Wedding Organizer*, which can help you keep track of all your wedding details in simple stunning style.

Your wedding flowers will give you enormous joy. You'll treasure the beauty they add to your celebration, and in the years to come, you'll always remember which blossoms you carried as you made your sweet journey down the aisle. With just a little knowledge and some imagination, you'll be better focused when it comes to choosing your blossoms and arrangements, and happier with the results.

Flowers inspire me every day. They are nature's perfect decorations—living examples of everything that is simple and stunning. Surround yourself with them at your wedding celebration, and luxuriate in their message of warmth, beauty, and love.

For an autumn wedding, create an heirloom-inspired farmhouse tablescape. White gourds, Queen Anne's lace, and creamy stock are nestled among glowing votives, square lanterns, and elegant taper candles.

stunningly SIMPLE

ten flower principles

Flowers are charming and lovely. Appreciating them is universal and effortless. But talking about them—with their complicated names, varying costs, and quirky seasonality—can be intimidating if you're not botanically inclined.

Not to worry! You don't need a degree in horticulture or a diploma in design. Whether you decide to create your own floral arrangements or to work with a pro, you can use this chapter for inspiration and good advice during the process.

As you're envisioning the blossoms, bouquets, centerpieces, and floral accents for your ceremony, keep in mind the ten flower principles you'll find in these pages. They'll help you streamline the floral design process and bring your perfect wedding vision to life. If you are considering creating your own wedding flowers, read the notes which follow, and make sure to plan well in advance so you'll have plenty of time to rest, relax, and enjoy every moment of your wedding week.

1. **Remember: Location equals inspiration.** Your setting should reflect the overall feeling you want your celebration to have, so look around and let your surroundings inspire you. In a formal hotel or historic space, keep floral designs soft and graceful (but not stuffy), and avoid designs that are too geometric or spare. If yours is a beach wedding, focus on low, windproof arrangements of natural grasses, or flowers floating in bowls filled with shells.

2. **Dream a little.** Before you worry about budgets or specifics, sit down with a cappuccino (or a glass of champagne) and a stack of magazines and books, and search out pictures of flowers you love. Look for appealing shapes, colors, and combinations. Create a file to keep track of what you like, and be sure to save some examples of flowers or arrangements you *don't* like. Share these pictures with prospective florists to help streamline your communications.

3. **Don't forget: Flowers are like wine.** Have you ever been intimidated by a giant wine list in a restaurant? The possibilities can seem endless. Like wine, flowers come in a complex and vast array, but ultimately,

flowers—and wine—are meant for our enjoyment. Remember that when you find yourself overwhelmed with too many details or options.

4. **Get in the mood.** Come up with several adjectives you'd use to describe the way you want your wedding flowers to feel. Ethereal and romantic? Spicy and passionate? Modern and monochromatic? Whimsical and organic? Keep these words in your flower file and share them with your florist. Hint: Chances are these descriptive words will apply to your whole celebration, so feel free to use them when speaking with caterers, musicians, and other wedding professionals throughout the process!

5. **Hire a "fresh" florist.** Fresh-thinking, that is. The best florists love to come up with creative ways to help you bring your dreams to life. From your very first meeting, you should feel comfortable with and inspired by your chosen florist.

6. **Celebrate the season.** Choose blossoms that are in season. Flowers, like fruits and vegetables, come and go throughout the year, so acquaint yourself with what's "in." Roses and orchids, for example, are available almost year-round, whereas dahlias, sweet peas, peonies, and hyacinths are found only during specific months. By choosing seasonal blossoms, you'll not only save money, you'll also assure that you'll be able to get your flowers every year on your anniversary.

For an ethereal, romantic look, alternate arrangements from table to table. These crystal bowls hold two variations on a classic bridal theme: white ranunculus paired with Queen Anne's lace, and open White Majolica spray roses.

7. **Get more with less.** Two of the biggest (in both senses of the word) mistakes in wedding design include overdecorating the ceremony and creating overly large reception table centerpieces. Bigger is not always better, and less is nearly always more. Choose flowers, greens, or leaves with beautiful forms, and show them off a few at a time for a simple, stunning effect.

8. **Keep in mind: Simple is as easy as 1-2-3.** In most cases, you'll make a more powerful visual statement if you limit the number of colors in any one floral arrangement (and in any one room) to three or fewer. Do mix shades of one color (pale peach to deep orange, for example) and feel free to vary your floral colors from room to room if you like.

9. **Don't be deceived: Simple is not always cheap.** A single stem of *Cymbidium* orchids can cost as much as a dozen roses. A mass of green hydrangeas imported from South America is strikingly simple, but no bargain. Thinking simple is about limiting the number of different elements, materials, and colors you combine to achieve the most powerful effect.

This ultra-modern centerpiece features less than a dozen stems of gorgeous, affordable irises, including the fresh petal napkin accents. And the easy-to-carry vases could be given to guests as favors at the party's end.

10. **Think like a Boy Scout.** Their motto, "Be prepared," works wonders for wedding design in general and for flowers specifically. Look at a sample of your reception centerpieces in advance of the wedding. Ask your florist to show you a photo or to create a mock-up for your approval. That way you can approve or alter floral choices and items such as color and composition before the big day.

notes for florally inclined brides

Are you a budding floral designer? A garden maven? Do your friends ask you to decorate their cocktail gatherings and dinner parties with charming arrangements because you "know how to put things together"?

If so, you might be considering the idea of creating your own floral arrangements for your wedding. It's a wonderful thought: you gathering armfuls of your favorite blossoms and quickly tucking them into glass bowls or compotes. It seems so easy and like such a great way to personalize and to save money. But beware:

A florist makes it look easy. This seemingly casual garden arrangement was days in the making. Purchasing, feeding, and conditioning flowers to peak bloom, painting and lining the basket with plastic and foam, and, of course, the design, are all part of the process.

Producing flower arrangements for a wedding—even a small one—and especially for *your* wedding, can be difficult, tedious, and time-consuming.

Think carefully about whether you really want to spend the days leading up to your celebration filling buckets, cleaning roses, and transporting heavy boxes full of arrangements to your ceremony or reception. Unless your wedding flowers are extremely simple or you have a flower shop and staff to help, hiring a professional florist is the best bet. Save yourself precious time and unnecessary trouble.

But for those ambitious, artistic brides who aren't daunted by these warnings, here are some helpful inside tips.

HINTS FOR ARRANGING YOUR OWN WEDDING FLOWERS

- **Choose sturdy blossoms.** Avoid delicate wildflowers or temperamental blooms such as hydrangeas, poppies, sweet peas, and lilacs. Opt for sunflowers, dahlias, or other strong varieties.
- **Buy conditioned flowers.** This is like asking your butcher to quarter a chicken for you. Prepping flowers takes time and knowledge, as many varieties require special care. Ask your local flower shop to prepare buckets of your blooms so you know they'll be in great shape and ready to arrange.
- **Stick to a few types of flowers.** Avoid complicated combinations. Simplifying your designs will speed up the time it takes to make your arrangements.

- **Use plants.** Plants are by nature generally more hearty than cut blooms. You can plant centerpieces or accents early in the week of your wedding and have plenty of time for your rehearsal dinner and last-minute errands.

- **Make a sample.** At least a few weeks in advance of the big day, make a test arrangement with your chosen flowers and containers to confirm the number of buds you'll need. Look at height (to avoid blocking dinner conversation), shape, and proportion to the container. Leave the arrangement overnight and watch for changes the next day. You don't want cloudy water, wilted foliage, or unexpected growth (tulips, for example, grow even when cut) on your special day.

- **Don't wait till the last minute.** Have all your flowers ready to arrange by the morning prior to your wedding day. Bouquets should be tied with raffia or taped with waterproof floral tape and left in glasses of water until the morning of your wedding, when you can finish them with ribbons or trim.

- **Get help.** There are lots of small tasks involved in making flower arrangements, such as packing, moving vases, the actual arranging, cleaning up, and removing rubbish. Ask a friend or a member of your bridal party to be your assistant.

Plants are an easy do-it-yourself option. Inexpensive daffodils repotted into moss-lined glass cylinders would make wonderful centerpieces, escort cards, or guest favors.

the money TREE

flower advice and budget

When you're planning your wedding, you'll likely find that the things you want and need, in general, are more expensive than you had anticipated. Most people who are not event planners have never hired a swing band or ordered engraved invitations with hand-lettered envelopes, and the going rates can seem sky-high.

Budgeting for wedding flowers and décor can be especially confusing and unpredictable, as there is no set cost for any given design element. Varying designers and markets, even nature—just about anything—can affect the price of wedding flowers.

The fact is, wedding décor budgets can grow like weeds in the garden—if you don't stay on top of them, they can quickly get out of control! So use this chapter as a reference when putting together your flower budget. It will help you focus and prepare. If you take time now to get organized before you contact florists for proposals and quotes, it will simplify the whole process.

financing your flowers

Assign a budget for blossoms when you're putting together your wedding numbers. Depending upon your decorative choices, flowers and other items (such as table linens and props) can cost between 5 percent and 25 percent of your overall budget. Think about your priorities: If you're a flower fanatic with a fancy for lush masses of poppies or peonies, you'll want to take that into account. If you're a minimalist, you can get away with less.

- **Know what you need.** Make a checklist before talking to prospective florists. Note the major things you know you need. Take into account the size of your wedding party, as you'll likely want bouquets for your bridesmaids, lapel flowers for the gentlemen, and even a toss bouquet for yourself, if you're planning on partaking in that tradition. Consider which flowers you want to adorn your ceremony, too. For the reception, estimate the number of tables you'll need to decorate, and consider whether you'll need an arrangement for your escort card table or any buffets or bars.

- **Focus your flower funds.** What detail is most important to you? Is it a particular flower type? A

favorite color? Or simply an overall feeling or ambience? Be as specific as possible, and communicate your priorities to your florist. A professional can help you create the look you want and suggest substitutions wherever your budget requires.

- **Compare your options.** Get written proposals and estimates from at least two or three florists so you can see where costs differ. Make sure you're comparing the same list of items, and that delivery, tax, and any other charges are included in the proposal.

pruning your blossoming budget

- **Look at your location.** Many wedding venues, such as restaurants, hotels, banquet facilities, and private clubs, have a florist on staff who provides flower arrangements on a weekly or daily basis. Inquire as to whether any arrangements will be in place on your wedding date, and if so, find out whether you can request specific colors or flowers to coordinate with your wedding.

- **Stay seasonal.** If you've chosen a date and location, use flowers that are readily available rather than fancy imported blooms. Peonies, like many other special flowers, including dahlias, cosmos, lilies of the valley, amaryllises, ranunculuses, and

Seasonal flowers benefit your budget. This autumnal bouquet combines Circus and Sari roses with miniature calla lilies. Textural green berzelia lanuginosa add a rustic touch.

hyacinths, are only in season during certain months and can be unavailable—or a lot more expensive—in between growing periods.

- **Don't overdecorate your ceremony.** Think of your flowers as a tribute, not as an opportunity for excess. Create a beautiful backdrop for your vow space, and place something special at the beginning of the aisle to mark your entrance. Avoid sight-blocking arrangements at all costs.

- **Banish random décor.** Stay away from pedestals and small arrangements placed here and there. These random elements tend to disappear in a party space. Instead, concentrate on areas that are focal points (fireplaces, entrances, escort card table, and so on) and create something spectacular there.

- **Think double-duty.** Design clever details you can use twice. *Don't*, however, move arrangements from your ceremony to your reception if it will make for awkward timing or will impact your guests ("Excuse me, Aunt Betty, can you move so the florist can grab that aisle marker?").

- **Remember, some holidays affect flower prices.** In general, flowers (and sometimes design-labor

These charming Duet dahlias are actually doing triple duty, first as escort cards, then as centerpieces (guests carry the vases to their tables), and finally as favors to take home at the party's end. Gerbera daisies, tulips, or poppies would work well, too.

charges) are more costly around Valentine's Day, Mother's Day, Christmas, and New Year's Eve.

- **Use masses of inexpensive flowers.** A giant bundle of white carnations or chrysanthemums can rival a similar rose arrangement when artfully crafted. These classic, underappreciated blooms come in many stunning varieties. Other great bargains include sunflowers, baby's breath, tulips, and alstromerias.

- **Create centerpieces with plants.** Small pots of herbs or beautiful leafy hostas or crotons; silver bowls containing azalea topiaries; or square planters holding single orchids—all of these are generally less expensive than most cut-flower arrangements, and charmingly unexpected.

- **Make bouquets smaller.** Petite posies are timeless and chic, whether made from a few stems of modern calla lilies or a handful of whimsical wildflowers.

- **Don't use flowers.** Create your centerpieces from candles or branches. If you're celebrating in a restaurant, make your décor a feast for all the senses: Cluster bread baskets and snacks (cheese, olives, grapes) in the center of the table, and add a few candles for a soft glow.

Support your local farmers' market in simple stunning style—buy bulk seasonal fruits and vegetables and arrange them in bushel baskets, metal pails, or modern boxes like these. Then bestow the bounty upon your guests or donate extras to a food charity.

Instead of decorating all your tables with identical floral arrangements, create budget-friendly, visually appealing variations-on-a-theme. Here, we've alternated gardenesque bouquets of Lemoncello spray roses, green cockscomb, chamomile, and hypericum berries with simple clusters of classic candle lanterns.

smart flower substitutes

When you visit a flower shop, do you find yourself drawn to the most expensive blooms in the window? Don't despair! Many beautiful, expensive flowers have more modest cousins or counterparts that, when arranged with panache, can create a similar mood and style without breaking the bank. Here are some ideas.

ROSES

Plump, romantic garden roses are super seasonal. They can also be temperamental and quite pricey. If you like that blown-open look, try other more readily available varieties of greenhouse-grown roses.

- **Allure** is a soft, fragrant, lavender rose.
- **Ambiance** features yellow and pink hues and is fluffy and dramatic.
- **Titanic** and **Toscanini** are pale pink giants.
- **Sahara** has a café-au-lait coloring and an "antique" look.
- **White Majolica** is a wide-blooming spray rose with garden rose style.

These lush rose arrangements are made from showy greenhouse-grown varieties, which are generally less expensive (and more readily available) than garden roses. From left to right: Circus, Ambiance, and Sombrero.

There are thousands of lily varieties in a wide range of colors and prices. If you're considering lilies for your celebration, keep the following tips in mind.

- **Casablanca** is a giant, fragrant white Oriental Lily variety with a high price tag. If you love their showy style and perfume, use a few blooms in key places, and accent with less expensive Asiatic varieties, also available in white.

- In general, **Asiatic Lilies** are smaller than Oriental varieties, but they have more blossoms per stem and are more affordable.

- **Miniature white calla lilies** cost the same as or more than the classic larger calla varieties. These beauties offer big value in both centerpieces and large arrangements.

fabulous fillers

- If you want to create a passionate centerpiece of red roses, but you don't want to go broke in the process, revise your recipe to include half the number of perfect red roses, and substitute deep red carnations, dahlias, or smaller red spray roses for the other half. You'll achieve the same mood, add depth and texture to your arrangement, and save money. Avoid using greenery or other fillers if you want the most powerful visual impact. This concept also works well with white flowers.

- Consider using fruits as wonderful, economical filler for gorgeous, feastlike centerpieces. You can add grapes, limes, lady apples, miniature pears, or plums to your arrangements. Work with what's seasonal and readily available.

- Surround smaller centerpieces with a tailored "collar" of inexpensive leaves. Arrange just a few roses, tulips, dahlias, or other pretty flowers in a small vase. Tuck leaves around the rim of the vase to create a cuff that cradles the flowers, adding a finished look for less. *Galax* and lemon leaves are available year-round, while oak, maple, and pear are perfect in autumn.

- Use moss or wheat grass as a foundation for your decorations. Fill pretty baskets, pails, bowls, or boxes with either of these natural elements, which are available at your florist or garden center. If your containers are deep, start with a lining of foam or newspaper as a base. Then place just a few blooms in plastic water tubes and tuck them into the grass or moss.

Where not to scrimp: your bouquet. Every bride should indulge herself with her favorite flowers. Here, Bianca roses are nestled among lisianthus, miniature calla lilies, and blushing brides.

flower moods
FOR LESS

If you like this . . .	Consider this. . .
Delphinium	Snapdragon, Stock, Larkspur
French Tulip	Giant Calla Lily
Hydrangea	Carnation, Azalea, Dahlia
Lady's Mantle	*Bupleurum*
Lilac	Stock, Larkspur
Orchid	Iris, Gloriosa Lily
Peony	Dahlia, Spider Chrysanthemums
Queen Anne's Lace	Baby's Breath
Rose	Lisianthus, Tulip, Carnation
Stephanotis	Bouvardia
Miniature Calla Lily	Ornithogalum
Poppy	Gerbera Daisy
Gardenia	Rose

They're both gorgeous. Which one is more expensive? Substitute ruffly, low-cost carnations (right) for temperamental, high-priced hydrangea (left), and you'll save a bundle.

hiring the FLORIST

Florists today aren't always just floral decorators. In addition to making bouquets, centerpieces, and other arrangements with beautiful blossoms, many offer other design services. They might provide rental or custom table linens and chair covers, special candles or props, and even lighting design to accent your party.

Use your florist as a resource. Because they are designers, floral professionals often have suggestions for creative ways to use your space, and they may have worked in your wedding venue previously. They also might have clever ideas for other design-related details, such as invitations, place settings, and escort cards, which can add wonderful layers to your overall wedding design.

Hiring a florist can seem difficult if you don't consider yourself a "flower person" or feel you don't have an eye for design. But you can keep it simple. Follow these tips—they'll make it easier for you to communicate with florists you're considering. Take the

time to ask the questions listed, and make sure you're happy with the answers. The right florist will help you grow your wedding vision from a small seed in your imagination to a perfect celebration in full bloom!

To find talented, respected florists in your area, ask people you know and trust. Friends, family, colleagues—almost everyone is involved in a wedding at some point, so inquire for tips and advice. Bridal or local magazines can be good resources for the top designers in your region. Look around in hotels, shops, and restaurants. When you see an arrangement that is appealing to you, ask someone in charge, "Who is your floral designer?"

When you've come up with a few solid professionals, make contact. Call first, and discuss the items covered below. Once you've narrowed down your prospects, meet with any serious candidates so you can look at photos or sample arrangements and determine if you're compatible.

what to tell prospective floral designers

- **Important details:** Give the date, time, and location for both your ceremony and your reception. Mention this first to make sure your prospective florist is available.

- **How you found them:** Some florists offer a discount or waive certain fees if you were referred by another client or by a particular caterer or venue.

- **Facts about your celebration:** Start with the size of your wedding party (bridesmaids, groomsmen, ushers, flower girls, ring bearers, and so on) and the number of guests you expect for the ceremony and reception.

- **Basic information about your wedding venue:** This includes the "flow" or movement of guests from one space to another, table sizes and shapes, and decorative focal points such as fireplaces or dramatic staircases. Giving the basics will help convey your overall vision of your wedding, and will ensure an accurate budget quote. Have a checklist handy during your discussions (see the chapter titled The Money Tree and my *Simple Stunning Wedding Organizer* for help creating a checklist).

- **At least five adjectives describing the ambience you'd like to create:** *romantic, classic, elegant, vintage,* and *etheral,* for example. Words that define your wedding style will help launch design discussions in the right direction—and pictures are even more helpful, so bring along books or magazines.

Florists often have access to pretty candleholders and fine linens. They can even help with packaging for guest favors, like these leaf-wrapped tea bags, each finished with an orchid.

- **Your general budget for flowers:** Do some research before calling florists for quotes so you'll know what to expect. Most good florists have design options for a range of budgets, and if you let them know in advance what you want to spend, they can tailor their creative thinking—and their prices—to your needs. If a florist has a minimum or cannot work within your budget, it's best to find out before you spend a lot of time discussing specifics.

- **Your favorite flowers and colors:** The more precise you can be, the better. "Hot pink" or "baby pink" is easier to picture than just "pink." Also, if you know the names of flower varieties you love, such as Bianca roses or Green Goddess calla lilies, share those as well. And if you're unsure, ask which flowers will be in season at the time of your wedding.

- **Anything else you're already sure of:** Share details concerning conditions in place at your ceremony and/or reception sites or other issues you're aware of (timing constraints, other weddings that day, candle regulations, insurance requirements, and so on). Also mention any floral allergies or aversions you or any wedding party members have. This will help everyone avoid unpleasant surprises later. You'll also discover up front whether there will be any additional costs.

Show your florist photos or samples of your tabletop details, such as china and crystal. This will help insure that your floral decorations harmonize with your overall look.

questions TO ASK

A PROSPECTIVE FLORAL DESIGNER

- Are you available on our date? If so, will you have other weddings that day?

- Have you worked at our ceremony site before? Our reception venue? If not, would you be willing to visit our location(s) to discuss design?

- How are your fees structured?

- Can you provide what we need within our budget?

- Do you offer other services besides floral design?

- Do you have a Web site or portfolio we can view?

- Who would be on-site to set up decorations for our wedding?

- May we have a written proposal with an estimated budget for each area of décor, as well as a list of terms and policies?

- Could we speak to some couples you've worked with?

- How does the process of working with you begin? What are the next steps?

the best BOUQUETS

Bridal party, or "personal," flowers are steeped in tradition going almost as far back as wedding celebrations themselves. In ancient Greece, brides and grooms were adorned with festive garlands and heralded with the tossing of petals.

The first bridal bouquets were small gatherings, or nosegays, of fragrant herbs and flowers (and even garlic!) carried by the bride to ward off evil spirits who might wish to do her harm. The bouquet tradition evolved to include the bride's attendants, or maids, who would carry posies to confuse the evil spirits further by making it difficult to tell who was the bride.

Bridal bouquets became very popular in Victorian times, when specific flower varieties were used to send messages. Small wedding posies were assembled with serious consideration by brides who lived by the maxim "A flower speaks a thousand words." Rosemary for remembrance, ivy for devotion, roses for love—the list is long and detailed. But woe to the bride who hadn't read her floral dictionary (many homes had one as a reference)—some poor flowers were actually thought to bear negative messages or omens.

Luckily, today the floral world is a lush wedding garden ripe for the plucking, and personal flowers are chosen to match the particular style of a couple and the mood of their celebration.

Throughout the twentieth century, various styles of bridal bouquets went in and out of fashion, from lush "shower" bouquets with their wired flowers and trailing ribbons, to Miss America–style "arm" bouquets, to floral scepters, pomanders, and other trends. Nowadays, three types of bouquets stand out as the most popular styles:

1. **Hand-tied.** This is a very popular and versatile style for both brides and bridesmaids. Most hand-tied bouquets are designed to be carried in front, at waist level. They can be soft, loose gatherings of wild flowers, or tailored, sculpted arrangements with a more formal feel. Hand-tied bouquets can feature a mix of flowers, or just one variety. Generally, the stems are tied with a ribbon or raffia or even a swatch of fabric from the bride's dress. Smaller versions might be called posies, and hand-tied bouquets of fragrant blossoms are often called nosegays.

It takes a florist to create this seemingly simple bouquet. White Majolica spray roses are coaxed to perfect bloom and wired, with viburnum accents, to create a slight cascade.

2. **Cascading.** This elegant style has its roots in the tradition of the "showering" and "love-knot" bouquets, which featured ribbons tied into knots and studded with blossoms and leaves. Designed to be carried in front, cascading bouquets are soft and romantic. A cascade can consist of just one type of flower, such as flowing *Dendrobium* orchids, or a mix of greens and flowers. These bouquets can be expensive, as flowers must sometimes be hand-wired to achieve the waterfall-like effect.

3. **On-the-arm.** Generally, the arm bouquet is designed to accommodate bigger flowers or those with longer stems, such as calla lilies, larkspurs, and delphiniums. An on-the-arm bouquet is typically cradled in one arm. Stems might be wrapped in a simple satin ribbon or a band of lace or crystal trim.

choosing the bouquet that's right for you

- Look through magazines and books, and note photos of bouquets you find appealing.
- Think about your dress. If it has a lot of intricate patterning or dramatic details, consider a simple bouquet to balance your look. If it's more casual, choose loose, airy flowers to complement the style.

- Ask yourself how you feel about fragrance. Tell your florist if you (or your groom or maid of honor) have any allergies or aversions to fragrant flowers. During your ceremony, you'll prefer "I do" to "a-choo!"
- Avoid squishy berries, dyed flowers, and blossoms with pollen intact. These are dress stainers. If you want lilies or the like, just ask your florist to "de-pollinate" the stems in your bouquet.

- Choose care-free flowers. Gardenias, garden roses, and anemones are gorgeous, but they're not the sturdiest blooms, and you don't want browning or wilting flowers in your photos.

Orange Volcano ranunculus, white ranunculus, and hydrangea are tied with a two-tone ribbon braid (opposite).

creative bouquet
ACCENTS

- Tie a handkerchief that belongs to your mother or another special woman in your life around the stems. It may come in handy during your vows, for tears of joy or perspiring palms!

- Ask your florist to wire pretty beads or crystals into your bouquet. After the wedding, have them strung on a bracelet or pendant as a keepsake.

- Make an aromatherapy bouquet. Add relaxing lavender, refreshing scented geranium leaves, or invigorating rosemary to your flowers. This little touch will help soothe you all the way down the aisle.

- Fasten your flowers together with a band of rhinestones or a piece of antique lace, trim, or cord instead of a ribbon.

- Make a wish bouquet. Each bridesmaid writes a wish for you on a small piece of paper, and then folds the paper into a ribbonlike strip. Tie or pin the wishes into your bouquet for good luck. After the ceremony, take a moment to open and read each wish. Then save them for your scrapbook.

for your bridesmaids and other treasured women

With so many beautiful flowers and accents available for the ladies in your bridal party, you are limited only by your imagination. Loose gatherings of dune grasses, dahlias, or sunflowers; tailored bouquets of roses, orchids, or calla lilies; lush armfuls of hydrangeas or peonies—what's perfect for your wedding?

Think first about what you're wearing and carrying. Your bridesmaids' attire should harmonize in style and formality, and should coordinate (but not necessarily match) with your chosen palette. Once you've determined what your attendants will wear, use these next few tips to help you choose their flowers.

To create more visual "pop," look for flower colors and shades that complement, rather than match, your bridesmaids' dresses. For example, if they will wear hot pink, choose posies in the palest shade of pink to create depth and texture, or opt for orange, green, burgundy, or ivory blooms for more contrast. You want

This stunning bouquet is made from just one unusual element—ruffly ornamental kale (that's right, cabbage!) in variegated purple and green.

fail-safe color COMBINING

TIPS FOR FLOWERS AND CLOTHING

- Green looks good with any other color and also makes for a great bouquet on its own.

- Ivory is warmer and less modern than bright white.

- Blue is the hardest flower color to find.

- Texture comes from layering shades of the same color. Think: pale pink to magenta, lavender to deep purple, cream to cocoa.

- Color creates mood. For a softer ambience, choose softer shades: pastels, naturals, and whites. For a stronger visual effect, opt for stronger hues: fuchsia, tangerine, and apple-green, for example.

- Bouquets and attire benefit from the 1-2-3 principle. For a simple stunning look, each bridesmaid, with her dress and flowers, should sport no more than three colors.

the flowers to stand out and be seen against the dresses rather than disappear against a like background.

Think timeless: Simplicity never goes out of fashion. Stay away from architectural bouquets or gimmicky designs, and opt instead for flowers and styles that you'll still love when you look at your photos years from now.

Less can be more. A small posy of exotic red gloriosa lilies makes a big statement for a fashion-forward bride or her maids.

Nothing is sweeter or more joyful than the lovely young ladies who announce the bride's entrance adorned with floral head wreaths and baskets of petals. Remember the following points when planning for your flower girls:

● **Choose flowers that are age appropriate.** The youngest flower girls may not be comfortable with large head wreaths, and in fact, their hair might just be too fine to hold pins. Know what will work for your girls.

alternatives to BRIDESMAIDS' BOUQUETS

■ **Order posies instead of bouquets.** Petite bouquets are both chic and cheaper than their larger counterparts. Just five roses or tulips tied together with a satin ribbon makes a great accent for any bridesmaid.

■ **Think classic and creative.** Wrist corsages are less expensive than bouquets, easier to wear, and movie-star chic when beautifully designed. A single orchid or peony tied with a luxurious satin ribbon around a bridesmaid's wrist—what could be prettier?

■ **Pin flowers in their hair.** Instead of opting for big, pricey bouquets, which have a tendency to be abandoned post-ceremony, ask your florist to wire fresh or silk blossoms for your bridesmaids' hair. Pin them in just before photos or the ceremony and leave hands free for hugging and raising the roof.

- **Ask at your ceremony venue about tossing petals.** Some settings do not permit this tradition—inside or out—for various reasons, including messy cleanup, slipperiness, and carpet stains.
- **Include her in the rehearsal.** Make a mock-up of the basket and petals, and give your flower girl a chance to get comfortable with her role.
- **Do something different.** Instead of having your flower girl toss petals, give her a small basket of individual stems and let her present flowers to both mothers and to other special ladies seated on the aisle. This idea works best with flower girls who are a bit older, as they'll welcome the extra honor and responsibility.

HONORING YOUR MOTHERS AND OTHER CHERISHED WOMEN

Moms, grandmothers, and all the other fabulous women in a bride's life have never been more chic or lovely. And they all have specific opinions about where flowers fit in with their ensembles. Following are some fresh ideas you can suggest to your honored ladies:

- **Small, fragrant nosegays:** These are miniature bouquets, sometimes called tussie-mussies, made from fragrant flowers and herbs. You can make matching ones for all your special ladies, or feature their favorite flowers individually. Many women prefer these small bouquets to classic corsages, which can damage outfits when pinned to jackets or tops.

Choose unusual combinations and varieties. Pair frilly Cummings tulips with velvety dusty miller (opposite) or tuck exotic mini Cymbidium orchids between lavender lisianthus blooms (above).

- **Single stems:** Calla lilies, long-stemmed roses, orchids, and peonies have such elegant forms. Just a single blossom accented with ribbon makes a wonderful tribute. Take a moment to present each blossom to your treasured ladies, or have your flower girls deliver them on their way down the aisle.

- **Wrist corsages:** These are ever-glamorous, easy to wear, and inexpensive. A gorgeous wrist corsage is a fantastic way to celebrate the great women in your lives.

proper grooming

It is said that the groom's buttonhole flower, or boutonniere, stems from the armor of the jousting knights of yore, who would wear colorful blooms to proclaim their love for a certain sweetheart. But why do the gents of today wear their flowers on the left lapel? This detail may also pay tribute to the olden days. When sword-toting grooms kidnapped their chosen beloved, they would clasp their lady loves to their left side, while keeping their right free for fighting off other would-be husbands.

Thankfully, modern grooms wear lapel flowers simply to adorn their festive attire (no jousting required),

Opposite, from left: Nerine and bear grass; miniature calla lily with silver brunia; freesia and steel grass; *Phalaenopsis*; *Dendrobium* with hanging amaranthus.

and the options are endless. Flowers, herbs, twigs, acorns, grasses—anything goes for the stylish husband-to-be and his attendants. Following are some floral tips for the men in your wedding party:

- **Coordinate his flower with something from your bouquet.** In one of the sweetest wedding traditions of yesteryear, the groom's boutonniere was a blossom plucked from the bride's bouquet. Follow the same course with your attendants, coordinating the ladies and gentlemen, but make sure your groom stands out with a special bloom.

- **Order extras.** Ask your florist to make one extra boutonniere for your groom. He'll pin one on before the ceremony and save one in case of breakage or browning before or during the reception. It's also a good idea to order one extra boutonniere for the groom's attendants, just in case.

- **Use robust blooms in boutonnieres.** Roses, miniature calla lilies, and stephanotises are tried-and-true wedding blossoms. *Hypericum* berries, *Galax* leaves, and bear grass are hearty, earthy components. Orchids such as *Dendrobiums*, *Vandas*, and miniature *Cymbidiums* offer strong, stunning blossoms in lots of color choices.

- **Honor other special gentlemen, such as fathers and grandfathers, with lapel flowers as well.** These can simply match the groomsmen's boutonnieres, or they can vary slightly, but they should be coordinated with the overall look and should convey elegance and simplicity.

reverence & ROMANCE

ceremony decor

At your wedding ceremony, the moments will be filled with magic; the words and traditions will come to life in the realization of your dreams. It's the beginning of your marriage and the kickoff to the celebration you've spent so much time imagining and planning.

You in your dress, your wedding party decked out in their finest, your setting meaningful—even without any decoration, your ceremony would be beautiful. But adorning your vow space is a wonderful way to celebrate the occasion and to pay tribute to the importance of the day.

What you don't want or need is an overdecorated ceremony space. Think of any flowers or accents as a way to honor your church, temple, ballroom, or other space, and you'll be on the right track.

Whether you'll celebrate in a house of worship, a hotel ballroom, a modern loft, or an open field, use this chapter to help you envision and design perfect floral accents for your own magical trip down the aisle.

let your location inspire you

When choosing décor for your ceremony, allow your venue's inherent ambience to guide you. If you're taking your vows in an apple orchard, let nature do the decorating. Just add small baskets of apples to the aisle, or hang ribbons from the trees, and you're all set.

If your ceremony takes place in a church or temple, look to the architecture to guide you. Most houses of worship benefit beautifully with the placement of just a few special arrangements at the entrance, the start of the aisle, and flanking the vow space itself.

If you're getting hitched in a modern loft or hotel ballroom, decorating can be especially challenging. These are often spare or neutral spaces designed for many uses. Pick a pretty window, fireplace, or corner as a backdrop, and create two to four dramatic arrangements to anchor your ceremony. Large branches and flowers or leaf designs will surround you with beauty, create visual focus in the room, and provide a stunning background for your wedding portraits.

This ceremony, set on the grounds of famed New York restaurant Blue Hill at Stone Barns, is a tribute to the natural setting. A canopy of curly willow branches holds local hydrangea, bittersweet berries, and springeri greens.

inside advice

- **Inquire whether other weddings will take place before or after yours at your ceremony location.** Other celebrations may restrict the time your florist has for delivery and setup, and you may be required to remove arrangements immediately after your service.

- **Consider whether you'd like to donate your wedding flowers as an offering to a house of worship or in memory of a loved one.** Ask a representative from your chosen setting about making arrangements if this idea appeals to you, then confirm with your florist that containers may be left on-site.

    If you cannot leave arrangements in the church, you could donate them to a local charitable organization. Ask your florist for recommendations, as they may have dealt with similar requests in the past. Certain hospitals and other organizations have restrictions on floral donations, so make plans in advance.

- **Decide if you want your ceremony décor transported to your reception.** Many wedding magazines recommend this measure as a way to save money, but it only works if there is enough time (and a guest-free route) to make the move. Note that extra delivery charges may apply.

In a church with a beautiful altar, you may only need to add a few accents, like these stunning classic urn arrangements of hydrangea and Queen Anne's lace.

A bittersweet berry welcome wreath (above) can be taken home and enjoyed for months after the wedding. Simple garlands of hearty carnations make romantic aisle accents (opposite).

your ceremony décor: simple and stunning

- **Adorn the entrance to your ceremony.** Add a garland, wreath, or a pair of topiaries as a romantic welcome for your guests. This will also make a great backdrop for photos as you exit for the reception.

- **Decorate the first few pews or rows on your aisle.** Mark these special seating areas with flower swags, bouquets, or buckets filled with wildflowers as a way to honor your families and loved ones.

- **Accent the beginning of your aisle with something pretty.** You could choose an arch draped with vines and blossoms, a gate covered in garlands, or two formal arrangements in classical urns. These accents will create a special entrance for you and your wedding party, and will also provide a festive background for all the pictures your friends, family, and photographers will snap as you float down the aisle.

- **Avoid large arrangements on your aisle.** These might block your friends' and families' view of the ceremony. No matter how charming it looks when they first walk in, your loved ones will be disappointed if they can't see you clearly.

- **Set a remembrance table with candles and flowers or petals.** Place it at the entrance to your ceremony or in your vow space to honor loved ones who can't be with you.

celebrate with branches

- Spring brings branches such as cherry, lilac, crab apple, and forsythia. Some, like lilac, are very fragrant, so be sure to tell your florist if you have allergies—or preferences for perfumy flowers.

- Summer features mostly leafy green branches, such as mountain laurel and camelia. Peegee hydrangea, a cone-shaped, rustic variety of the popular flowering bush, appears in some areas beginning in August.

- Mid to late autumn offers oak, maple, pear, and berry branches such as bittersweet, pyracantha, and ilex.

- Early winter is filled with evergreens like pine, fir, and juniper, while late winter offers spare, delicate branches such as quince and dogwood.

- Year-round best bests for nonleafy branches are birch and curly willow, which are beautifully simple on their own and make great foundations for "flowering" arrangements constructed by a designer.

- Not a branchy bride? Bamboo and giant palm leaves such as arecas and coco palms are striking floras that can be used to create a modern, tropical, or Asian-inspired ceremony. Ask your florist what's available in your area.

Coming soon to a branch near you: For this New York City loft celebration, we anchored the vow space with two modern columns holding spheres of flowering lilac.

where to SPLURGE

While you're planning your wedding, it can be hard to know where to place flowers and décor if you're looking at an empty ballroom, banquet hall, loft, or historic mansion. Generally you and your designer will visit the spot when it's free and undecorated, typically during daylight hours or between parties.

If possible, stop by your wedding venue when it's set up for an event. Most locations will accommodate such a request if you are considerate and quick about it. You can also ask to see photos of previous weddings and parties in the space to help inspire you and give you an idea of what works and what doesn't.

When planning floral room décor, look at each space's focal points. Is there a foyer with high ceilings where you might place your escort card table? Does the venue feature a prominent fireplace or staircase? If you're unsure about where to add décor, ask your designer or the reception site manager for advice. The best advice: Always splurge where it will pack the biggest punch.

create at least one "wow!" moment

The best way to envision your wedding is to walk through your space as if you were a guest. Pay attention to where your eye naturally travels, and look for the major details and architectural elements that should be highlighted. Rather than placing an abundance of little things here and there, focus on just a few key spots in your venue, and create something dramatic and spectacular in those areas. The following are some important places to consider:

● **Entrances.** If your venue is a private mansion or a space with its own entrance, consider decorating it with something festive to say "The party starts here!"

If you're celebrating at a banquet facility or hotel or another spot that may be hosting multiple events, skip decorating the main entrance, and focus on the entrance to your room or rooms.

Tented weddings often need a visual anchor to create an entrance, and if you'll be using multiple tents (for cocktails, dinner, and dancing, for example) you might want to flank each passageway with pairs of arrangements or flower garlands.

This barn reception offers a warm welcome of rustic, romantic garlands and overflowing floral urns, along with a table set with glasses of sparkling wine.

Fireplaces. If there is a fireplace in one of your rooms, chances are it's a focal point. Invite guests to gather round by decking it out in flowers, branches, plants, or candles. If your wedding takes place in a month when the fireplace won't be lit, ask permission to fill it and cover the mantel with candles. But do be careful not to place any flammable branches or decorations too close to candles or burning logs.

Large pieces of furniture. Antique tables, dramatic sideboards, shelving units—these all can be transformed into bountiful, rustic, feastlike displays or powerful modern geometric statements. After you take a look around, make sure to get permission before you plan any floral décor: Some venues have restrictions to protect valuable pieces. Also, consider placing cork pads or other liners under vases; make sure candles are under glass if dripping wax is unacceptable; and give your florist a written list of any restrictions that apply.

Escort card displays. Escort cards tell guests which table they'll be seated at for lunch or dinner. For all but the smallest or most casual weddings, escort cards are a necessary and considerate detail, as they let guests know you've considered their seating. Whether you decide to lay out your cards on a simple round table or to create a giant tree bedecked with ribbons holding hand-lettered envelopes, your escort card display will likely be a gathering point.

High ceilings and open spaces benefit from decorative drama. Orchid "trees" are fashioned from curly willow branches and *Dendrobiums* (above). Blue Hill at Stone Barns boasts a giant farmhouse table which becomes an eye-catching centerpiece for this restaurant reception (opposite).

For a holiday wedding, use pine, juniper, spruce, fir, or other seasonal boughs to decorate your fireplace mantel, and accent with snowflakes or festive ornaments.

fireplace décor

Many event venues, especially those set in historic spaces, feature large fireplaces as focal points, like this one at Manhattan's Westside Loft. A fireplace can make a perfect backdrop for your ceremony or cocktail hour (and your formal portraits), and you'll want to adorn it with beautiful accents.

Potted plants and greens are a wonderful, budget-friendly alternative to complicated fresh floral designs. Check your local garden center or flower shop for plants and foliage which are in season for your wedding, and look for plants you can take home after the celebration and plant in your garden or hang in your sunny windows.

You can create an over-the-top spectacular design for your fireplace without ever removing any of your plants from their plastic pots. Start with cascading ivy plants, like the ones pictured here, to create a foundation. Arrange the pots here and there along the mantel in natural groupings. Next, add plastic pots filled with vibrant, open roses in your chosen palette. Tip some of the pots sideways—if necessary, use foam to prop them up securely, and create an organic cascade of colorful blossoms to rival any garden.

escort card splurges

- **Decorate your escort card table with masses of a single type of flower.** Roses, hydrangeas, peonies, dahlias, even carnations—the drama is in the size and scale of this attention-getting arrangement. The taller, the better! Add a few candles and your lovely cards, and watch guests ooh and aah.

- **Design a walkway of fabulous garlands hanging from floor to ceiling.** Pin or tie your escort cards among the flowers, here and there, following the alphabet (first half on the left, second half on the right).

- **Make a musical arbor.** This idea is wonderful for a tented wedding or any celebration in a natural setting. Your florist creates an arbor or series of arches with curly willow and birch branches, with flowers and greens tucked in. From the branches, long ribbons dangle, each holding a single wind chime bearing guests' names. Just make sure you have a plan to cover the arbor in case of inclement weather.

- **Create a flower shop.** Turn your escort card table into a blossoming interactive space. Ask your florist to set up a special cart or stand in your cocktail hour area. Each guest visits the "shop" to pick up their escort card, which is tied to a single flower stem or small posy. Small vases at each place setting hold guests' flowers during dinner (instant centerpiece). At the end of the party, everyone gets an easily totable floral favor to take home.

- **Remember, simple does not mean cheap.** When you use just one or two elements in giant masses or dramatic ways, you create a luxury of simplicity that is both fabulous and festive.

  Nothing makes a more eye-catching arrangement than a collection of tall branches. Ask your florist what's in season for your wedding, and order a whole bale of them for the center of your escort card table. If you like, you can tie your escort cards to the branches with colorful ribbons for a uniquely festive escort tree. Just start at one point on the tree and work alphabetically all the way around. Better yet, ask your florist or a friend to hang them for you. Make sure to allow plenty of room for guests to move around the tree, and provide scissors (and a staff member) to make cutting down cards easy and effortless. One more hint: Avoid branches with pointy thorns, such as pyracantha and quince, and stay away from flowering pear branches—although they have fabulous white blossoms, they also have an unpleasant odor.

Cherry blossoms, harbingers of spring, are some of the most romantic of flowering branches. Towering over a simple arrangement of elegant candles and escort cards, they make a striking statement.

adorning THE TABLE

the freshest centerpieces

Centerpieces are often among the first decorative elements brides envision. After all, the tables they adorn will be home to friends and family (between dance sets, of course) for several hours, so they must be attractive and unique.

Perhaps you have always known you want simple silver bowls filled with ivory roses, blue hydrangeas, or pale pink peonies on every table at your wedding. But if you're a bride with lots of ideas or if your vision isn't yet fully formed, you may find yourself overwhelmed by all the possibilities and all the pictures you've saved in your flower file.

Instead of feeling lost, take a look at those photos of centerpieces you've marked or saved. Divide them into moods. You'll either find that they naturally fall into just one or two categories (classic or Zen, for example) or that they represent wide-ranging tastes.

Once you've identified the moods you like, think about your location and its environment. Chances are

good that one of your chosen moods will seem more harmonious with your setting than the others. Focus on that mood, but keep the other images for specific references to flower varieties and color.

If you're just not sure, take the whole file to your florist's shop or studio and get help. Remember to share any adjectives you've written down to describe how you want your celebration to feel. Most design pros will be able to pick up on which qualities you're responding to, and they can help you streamline your inspiration based upon the season, your budget, and your preferences.

a world of options

Centerpieces today can be colorful collections of just flowers (without greenery or filler flowers), or unusual, textured combinations of greens and leaves. They can be arranged in a single central vase, compote, or bowl, or be made up of complementary, separate components collected in unique ways.

Some centerpieces celebrate just one type of flower in modern, geometric arrangements or luscious groupings, while others feature a mix of blooms and other elements.

Smaller, more modular centerpieces are perfect for long or round tables. From left: stock, irises, peonies, snapdragons, and Queen Anne's lace.

Fruits and flowers are a classic combination, but vegetables have begun to make their way into creative centerpiece designs, as have other organic elements such as unusual succulents, decorative shells, and velvety moss.

Stones, sand, feathers, crystals, ribbons—you name it and it can be a part of a unique and festive table design for your wedding. Just keep in mind that limits are never a bad thing when *putting together* your chosen ingredients.

Keep the height of your arrangements in mind. Are the ceilings at your reception venue high enough to accommodate tall branches or large vases? Will guests be able to see each other across the table? Think about the scale and style of your party when you're planning your floral décor.

Also think about whether you want guests to be able to take centerpieces home at the end of the party, or whether you'll reuse any of the flowers for a post-wedding brunch the next morning. If so, make sure to confirm with your florist that vases and blooms are yours to keep, as some items may be considered rentals. If you do plan on moving arrangements to another location, appoint a friend to take care of transporting them and setting them up.

Tailor your centerpieces to your location. For a casual beach wedding, cluster candles and white anthurium blossoms among polished shells in aluminum trays.

simple stunning centerpiece inspirations

- Turn a wide glass cylinder or bowl upside down and use it as a pedestal for an understated centerpiece of plants, fruits, or floating flowers. The extra few inches of height will add drama to your tables and will allow more room for candles and glasses. Just be sure the combination is secure and stable enough to withstand gentle bumps to the table.

- Fill interesting containers with moss or grass and finish with just one dramatic flower. Depending on the size of your container and your flowers, one centerpiece might be enough for every table, or you might combine multiple containers in eclectic or modern gatherings for a more dramatic effect.

- Use cut orchids as "plants." Orchid plants can be expensive, so ask your florist to use cut *Dendrobium* orchids to create faux plants for your centerpieces. These blooms come in a variety of pretty colors, including green, white, and pink, and are generally available year-round. Your florist will use flower

Traditional centerpieces may hold seventy-five flowers or more. But look! Just six blooms of the unusual succulent echeveria make a strikingly beautiful, exotic centerpiece.

foam and bamboo or branches to anchor the blossoms, and might accent with moss or stones for a finished look.

- Buy showy, inexpensive plants and present them beautifully. Azaleas with their big blooms, colorful chrysanthemums, common ferns, even hydrangeas—all these make stunning centerpieces. Choose a special pot or planter for each, and let guests take them home as a living memory of your big day.

- Combine twigs or leafy branches and candles for a simple, elegant centerpiece. Arrange tall pillar candles in white, ivory, silver, or gold in the center of your tables, and place branches at the base of the candles. Do keep safety in mind: Avoid low votive candles, and keep branches away from flames.

- Give centerpieces a fresh twist. Submerge orchids underwater; bend pliant miniature calla lilies; wind grasses around inside vases for a unique, chic effect.

- For a more interesting visual effect, create varying floral arrangements for each of your tables, all in your chosen color palette. One table might feature yellow tulips; another could highlight lemony roses; and a third might showcase sunny daffodils, for example. To complete your table design, accent each napkin with a coordinating blossom.

Instead of big, space-eating centerpieces for already crowded bars, arrange small, moveable vases filled with unusual varieties, such as lady's slipper orchids and miniature calla lilies.

not just flowers: centerpiece alternatives

- **Use what you have.** If you're in a restaurant, ask the chef or manager to place a row of apples or pears down the center of narrow tables, and add tea lights or tall taper candlesticks as an accent. Better yet, create an edible centerpiece with small snacks: spiced nuts, dates, and dried fruits; or olives, breadsticks, and hunks of Parmesan cheese. This is appealing, practical, and economical. You'll not only save money on flowers, but you may even save on your menu as well!

- **Visit your farmers' market.** Boxes, baskets, or bowls of fruits and vegetables make colorful, vibrant table decorations. If you're serious food lovers or if you're celebrating on a farm, consider using different fruits or vegetables from table to table, and mark your escort cards "Orange," "Red Pepper," and "Carrot," for example, instead of "Table 1," "Table 2," and "Table 3."

- **Get crafty.** If you like to make things, consider creating your own centerpieces from feathers, picture frames, or holiday ornaments. Just allow yourself plenty of time, and make your designs nonperishable so you can have them finished well in advance of the big day.

- **Use guest favors as centerpieces.** If you plan to give bottles of wine or olive oil, jars of honey or jam, or other attractive objects as mementos, place one

Think out of the vase. For a winter reception, pair shimmering silver candles with ornaments and twigs (above). A summer wedding table might feature plums on a bed of ornamental cabbage (opposite).

for each guest or couple in the center of the table, tied with a bow or tag or wrapped in a pretty package. This also works well with candy favors or cupcakes, which can be placed on cake stands or pedestals for a charming display. Accent your gift centerpiece with clusters of votives or tea lights for a romantic glow.

Covering containers with special papers is a great way to transform an everyday vase or can into a unique object.

container workshop

Classic mint julep cups and silver Revere bowls. Gracious ceramic pots, aluminum buckets, and casual planters. Fancy rented candelabra and crystal bowls. Inexpensive clear and frosted glass, even plastic. There are endless options for flower vessels to suit your wedding style.

You can dress up a simple container in lots of easy ways. A band of ribbon or a swatch of lace makes a great accent, as do sturdy leaves such as calathea and monstera, which can be wrapped around the outside of a vase or used as a chic lining inside a glass container. You might add charms, monograms, or antique buttons to your vases as a personal touch.

Ask your florist to suggest interesting container ideas, or visit your local craft store for inspiration. In general, double-stick tape and spray adhesive are great items to have on hand for this type of do-it-yourself project, as are decorative scissors, raffia, and assorted ribbons.

idea

Host a "cover girl" party. Invite your bridesmaids and friends to help you customize gorgeous containers. Use maps, doilies, moss, or papier-mâché to create one-of-a-kind vessels for your wedding centerpieces or cocktail arrangements.

accent on DETAILS

Flowers are wonderful in grand arrangements that can be appreciated for their scale and drama, but with their individual beauty and their inspiring forms, they can also be perfect accents for some of the smaller details at your wedding celebration.

- **One of the easiest ways to dress up a simple table setting is to add a single blossom to each guest's napkin.** Choose a flower that matches your chosen theme, and opt for hearty blooms that can remain out of water for a few hours without wilting. *Dendrobium* and *Cymbidium* orchids, roses, giant spider chrysanthemums, dahlias, and daisies are all good candidates. Avoid delicate blooms such as sweet peas, lilies of the valley, and peonies, unless they can be placed in water until the very last minute.

- **Herbs and grasses** are also great accents for your place settings. Ask your caterer or florist to wrap each napkin with a stem of fresh rosemary or bear grass, or tuck a sprig of lemon thyme into a napkin with a pocket fold.

Napkin floral accents such as the iris petals and *Dendrobium* blossom pictured above are elegant and economical. A single stem of *Dendrobium* adds a soft touch to a rented chair (opposite).

- **Miniature wreaths** made from flowers, greenery, or twigs make lovely accents for the chairs at your head table.

- **Fragrant blooms are charming** for the ladies' room and men's room. Gardenia, stock, lilac, and tuberose are all sweet-smelling options.

- **Green leaves make great gift wrap.** Swath your guest favors in pretty ti leaves—they're strong, pliant, and inexpensive.

- **Preserved leaves serve well as escort cards,** and are readily available at craft stores. Write your guests' names with a decorative pen, and arrange the leaves on trays or "scatter" them (alphabetically, of course) on a long table.

- **Fresh, edible pansies, chrysanthemums, roses, or nasturtiums** make a great alternative to expensive sugar flowers for your wedding cake. Serve slices of the cake garnished with petals and a sweet sauce. Likewise, you can add edible flowers to hors d'oeuvres, salads, soups (see page 90), or other dishes for a festive botanical flourish. Ask your caterer to freeze rose buds in ice cubes and serve them with signature cocktails featuring floral-infused syrups or waters.

- **Seed packets** are readily available on the Internet, and many can be personalized as living guest favors for guests to plant in their home gardens.

- **A favorite floral motif used throughout your celebration** will tie everything together beautifully. Olive branches, tulips, jasmine, or roses—choose one variety and feature it on invitations, programs, and menu cards.

High-tech flora: Bakers now have the ability to "print" a floral pattern on your wedding cake (left). A floral motif is a wonderful accent for invitations, programs, and other printed materials (opposite).

TOGETHER WITH THEIR FAMILIES
MISS JACQUELINE CRAWFORD BRESSON
AND
MR. LAWRENCE ROBERT NOLAN
REQUEST THE PLEASURE OF YOUR COMPANY
AT THEIR MARRIAGE
SATURDAY, THE TENTH OF JUNE
AT THREE O'CLOCK
THE CHARLES CARROLL HOUSE
ANNAPOLIS, MARYLAND

DINNER AND DANCING TO FOLLOW

MR. & MRS. IAN MORRIS

KINDLY REPLY BY
THE TENTH OF MAY

SAVE THE DATE
THE TENTH OF JUNE

JACKIE BRESSON
AND
LARRY NOLAN
ARE GETTING MARRIED

ANNAPOLIS, MARYLAND

JACKIE & LARRY

LOBSTER NAPOLEON
ARTICHOKE, PURPLE POTATOES & CHEDDAR PASTRY

SEED-ENCRUSTED FILET OF BEEF
WITH SHALLOT SAUCE
BUTTERNUT SQUASH SPAETZLE
& HARICOTS VERT

WEDDING CAKE
WITH CRÈME ANGLAISE & FRESH RASPBERRIES

ANNAPOLIS, MARYLAND

flowers BY MOOD

Flowers have individual "personalities." Some, like garden roses and viburnums, are soft and romantic. Others, like calla lilies and freesias, are linear and crisp. Daisies are casual and fun, while peonies are ruffly and ultrafeminine. Heliconias and proteas say, "I'm exotic!" What's your flower personality?

Use the following four charts to help identify flowers that harmonize with your wedding style. There are hundreds—even thousands—more varieties to consider, and many of the flowers pictured are available in a number of different colors, so be sure to ask your florist for more information and recommendations.

Of course, flowers can't be unequivocally categorized. So use this guide as a starting point, for inspiration. Think about what you like (and what you don't like). Then choose flower combinations that appeal to you. Mix and match styles for an eclectic look, or design different moods for your ceremony and your reception.

Whimsical, airy, lush, and soft—these flowers inspire dreams of fragrant fields and romantic paths. Whether arranged alone or in ethereal combinations, the blossoms pictured here are feminine and festive.

1. Larkspur

2. Waxflower

3. Dahlia

4. Sunflower

5. Hydrangea

6. Toscanini Rose

7. Snapdragon

8. Peony

9. Stock

10. Ambiance Rose

11. Hyacinth

12. Delphinium

13. Cestrum

denesque

5
6
7
8
9
10
11
12
13

Unique forms, clean lines, and less foliage make these blossoms ideal for striking geometric arrangements or tailored groupings.

1. Silver Brunia

2. Minerva Amaryllis

3. Hanging Amaranthus

4. Horsetail Bamboo

5. *Cymbidium* Orchid

6. Jade Rose

7. *Dendrobium* Orchid

8. Super Parrot Tulip

9. Calathea Leaf

10. Nerine

11. Bells of Ireland

12. Ornithogalum

13. Eucharist Lily

14. Green Goddess Calla Lily

15. Lady's Slipper Orchid

16. Bear Grass

17. Schwarzalder Miniature Calla Lily

18. *Phalaenopsis* Orchid

19. Echeveria

20. Freesia

21. Gerbera Daisy

SIMPLE STUNNING WEDDING FLOWERS

modern

Spicy and funky, chic and unexpected, these bold blooms are often best highlighted alone for their stunning forms and colors, or used in simple combinations that allow their beauty and unmistakable style to shine through.

1. Anthurium

2. Hanging Heliconia

3. Pincushion *Protea*

4. Monstera Leaf

5. Chili Pepper

6. Ornamental Pineapple

7. Ginger Flower

8. Pandanus Leaf

9. *Vanda* Orchid

10. Areca Palm

11. Upright Heliconia

12. Crocosmia

13. Psittacorum

14. Song of India

exotic

5 6 7 8 9 10 11 12 13 14

These beautiful blossoms have graced many a wedding ceremony and celebration throughout the ages. Stephanotis, for example, is considered a good-luck charm for weddings. Depicted here in whites, some of the blossoms are available in other colors or variations.

1. Calla Lily
2. Bianca Rose
3. Stock
4. Stephanotis
5. Cheers Tulip
6. Baby's Breath
7. Gardenia

8. Lisianthus
9. Ranunculus
10. Lily of the Valley
11. Miniature Calla Lily
12. Vendela Rose
13. Queen Anne's Lace

classic

acknowledgments

There are so many kind and talented people to thank for their help in making this book possible. Why not say it with flowers? To my publisher, Leslie Stoker, I present overflowing armfuls of fresh French lavender tied with fine silk ribbon, in thanks for her unwavering devotion to creating excellent books. For my bright and bubbly editor, Jennifer Levesque, I offer a giant basket filled with heirloom garden roses in vibrant hues with as many thank-yous as stems for all her efforts on my behalf.

When it comes to Joy Tutela, my agent and angel, only rare Italian poppies in full bloom will do, accompanied by a wheelbarrow of gratitude. For William Geddes, my super-talented photographer, whatever his wife likes—and lots of it! And for Susi Oberhelman, whose gorgeous graphic design for this book so beautifully expresses the simple stunning look, a colorful blossom for every special detail she designed.

Twenty bushels of sunflowers to Lance York, Linda Lieberman, Errin Verdesca, and everyone at Tri-Serve Party Rentals for their generosity and assistance. But Lance, you have to send a TriServe truck to pick them up.

To each and every member of my production and studio staff, a lush, perfect bouquet which they do not have to make for themselves. Special and heartfelt thanks to Lauren Wells, Mats Nordman, Brett Underhill, and Tuyen Lam, along with Anibal Polo, Jeremy Norman, Paco Rodriguez, and Aure Morales.

To John "Johnny C" Kiamos and all the great guys at Associated Cut Flowers, who are already up to their telephones in bountiful blossoms, extra large bottles of scotch which they are not required to share. To Gus Theofanis and Eddie Marquez of U. S. Evergreen, whose lives are chock-full of plant material, how about a few well-deserved days off, in a row? Same goes for Sabir and Mokaram Tahherly at Jamali Garden Supplies, along with all the other hard-working early risers at New York's Flower Market, including Gary Page, Lauren Page, and Richard Moore of G Page Flowers and Tom of Caribbean Cuts.

I would like to give my dear, lovely sister Sara an exact replica of every bouquet she clasped on the numerous days when she modeled for this book. And to my brother David, an entire field of flowering sage in thanks for all the wisdom and good advice he has shared with me.

resource guide

PAGE 2:

Chair cover: Magnolia Linens
www.magnoliasgroup.com

Dress: Kleinfeld
www.kleinfeldbridal.com

PAGE 7:

Dress: Kleinfeld
www.kleinfeldbridal.com

PAGE 8:

Votives, metal vase, tray, and
hanging lanterns:
Jamali Garden Supplies
www.jamaligarden.com

Candle lanterns:
TriServe Party Rentals
www.triservepartyrentals.com

Candelabra: Chelsea Marketplace
www.chelseamarketplace.com

Mini white gourds:
U. S. Evergreen, New York City
212.741.5300

Location: Blue Hill at Stone Barns
www.bluehillstonebarns.com

Stunningly Simple:

PAGE 10:

Vases: Jamali Garden Supplies
www.jamaligarden.com

PAGE 13:

Cut crystal vase:
Chelsea Marketplace
www.chelseamarketplace.com

Table linen: Magnolia Linens
www.magnoliasgroup.com

Curtains: IKEA
www.ikea.com

PAGES 14–15:

Vases: Jamali Garden Supplies
www.jamaligarden.com

China, flatware, and linens:
TriServe Party Rentals
www.triservepartyrentals.com

PAGE 17:

Table linen: Magnolia Linens
www.magnoliasgroup.com

China and flatware:
TriServe Party Rentals
www.triservepartyrentals.com

PAGE 18–19:

Daffodil plants:
Holiday Foliage, New York City
212.675.4300

The Money Tree:

PAGE 24–27:

Vases: Jamali Garden Supplies
www.jamaligarden.com

PAGE 70:
Location: Blue Hill at Stone Barns
www.bluehillstonebarns.com

PAGE 73:
Candelabra: Chelsea Marketplace
www.chelseamarketplace.com

Ivy and rose plants: Fischer and
Page, New York City
212.645.4106

PAGE 74:
Curtains: IKEA
www.ikea.com

Cut crystal vase and candle holders:
Chelsea Marketplace
www.chelseamarketplace.com

Table linen: Magnolia Linens
www.magnoliasgroup.com

Adorning the Table:

PAGE 78-79:
China, crystal, flatware, and linens:
TriServe Party Rentals
www.triservepartyrentals.com

PAGE 80-81:
Trays, candles, and shells:
Jamali Garden Supplies
www.jamaligarden.com

Chairs, china, flatware, and linens:
TriServe Party Rentals
www.triservepartyrentals.com

PAGE 82-83:
China, crystal, flatware, and linens:
TriServe Party Rentals
www.triservepartyrentals.com

Metal planters:
Jamali Garden Supplies
www.jamaligarden.com

PAGE 85:
Pitcher, martini glasses, and tray:
TriServe Party Rentals
www.triservepartyrentals.com

Purple votive candles: West Elm
www.westelm.com

PAGES 86-87:
China, crystal, flatware, and linens:
TriServe Party Rentals
www.triservepartyrentals.com

Candles and ornaments:
Jamali Garden Supplies
www.jamaligarden.com

PAGE 89:
Papers: Paper Presentation
www.paperpresentation.com

Accent on Details:

PAGE 90:
Catering: Olivier Cheng Catering
www.ocnyc.com

PAGE 94:
Cake: Cheryl Kleinman Cakes
718.237.2271

PAGE 95:
All printed materials:
Russell Sloane
212.539.0184

Flowers by Mood:

PAGE 98:
Refer to page 17.

PAGE 100:
Refer to page 85.

PAGE 102:
Refer to page 38.

PAGE 104:
Refer to page 13.

index

(Page references in *italic* refer to illustrations.)

For more ideas and inspiration, visit us at www.karenbussen.com